Highway Heart

by

- David Jones -

David Jones was born in 1989 in Liverpool, which is still his home. He studied English Language and Literature at the University of Liverpool, before specialising in Renaissance and Eighteenth Century Literature. He started writing at an early age, and has published four poetry books (Could You Ever Live Without?, Love And Space Dust, Love As The Stars Went Out and Highway Heart) and a novella called Death's Door. He is also a filmmaker, playwright and actor, and is currently completing work on a full length novel.

For more information on the writer, visit: www.storydj.com, twitter @djthedavid or on Facebook at https://www.facebook.com/davidjoneswriter and @storydj Instagram. He also uploads weekly videos at http://www.youtube.com/storydj.

ISBN-13: 978-1532980237
ISBN-10: 153298023X

"The poem I never dared to write."

She is
What remains
When there
Is nothing
Else left.

She is the
Last dream before
The morning,
The final thought

Before the dark
And the
Last star in

The sky.

And I was
Never sure
Whether you
Were the
Lighthouse or
The storm.

The sunrise

Would look

So much

Better

Reflected

In your

Eyes.

And

In the end

All I learned

Was how

To be strong

Alone.

Love is simply
To know
The poison, but
Drink it
Anyway.

Why do I
Love you?
Why do the
Stars burn?

We both
Crave
Destruction and
Rebirth.

Autumn killed
The summer with
The softest kiss.

"And I waited."

- *A Three Word Short Story*

Back to
The stars.

Perhaps I'll
Find you
There.

Time:
The healer
And the
Killer.

I wanted
To explain, but
My soul was
Tied up in
Knots.

I fell for you
While the rain fell,
As eager for
You as the
Drops for the
Ground, but

The earth
Won't drown
In rain even

If I drown
In you.

I wondered how
She could be
The moon and

The sun, the sea
And the sky;
Heaven and
Hell.

Life went on,
But it was
Never the
Same
Again.

I looked into
Her eyes and knew:
The fire that
Warms can also
Destroy.

Perhaps we

Are wishing

For each other

Upon the

Same star.

Where are you?
The sky seems
Empty of stars

Tonight.

Goodbye.

I whispered to
The moon:

"I am going to
The stars.

Nowadays
All I hear
Are the unspoken
Words.

But who has not

Looked at the sea

And dreamt

Of feeding

Themselves to it?

She is

The poem

I never

Dared to

Write.

I still search
For you in
Every
Sunrise.

We were made
Of combustible
Materials:
The stuff of
Stars.

The moment
Our finger tips
Touched it was
Already the end.

One day
There will be
Nothing left
But
Stories.

It seemed like
The end but it was
Only the beginning:

Even the stars
Face destruction
Before rebirth.

What burning,
Dying stars
Gave birth to
Us?

What blazing
Death could
Light such a
Furnace of
Love?

Like a river
To the sea:
Love will find
A way.

It would be
Easier to survive
4am with
You.

Even after all
These years, the
Winter moon
Still looks at the
Earth and wonders
If the summer
Will ever
Return.

I looked up to
The stars and
Wished, but
The universe did
Not answer,
And why

Would it? Those
Stars have
Long since
Died their deaths,
And the heavens

Will never speak.

Life is

A few important

Moments and

A long

Time to

Relive and

Regret.

I don't want
A glamorous
Tragedy, I
Want a boring
Happy
Ending.

I loved her

Too much, and
Everything
She touched

Turned to
Dust.

I let you grow
In my heart, but
The roots strangled
The life out
Of me.

I lived my

Life in the summer

Of a love

That burned

Far brighter

Than the sun.

Sometimes I
Speak to you
As if you are
Still here, I
Think it's called

Poetry.

A Haiku on Love.

Love is not first sight:
A moment revealed *by* time -
Love is a moment.

You are still in
My veins, somehow.
My heart is still
Pumping you
Out, my lungs
Still breathe you
In,

You are still
In every word
I write.

A Dialogue with a Black Hole in Outer Space.

I thought, if only I could cry I would feel better, but my eyes were like deserts. I tried to be God and make it rain, but there was nothing. There was such a universe of nothing. All those stars, those galaxies, those vast portions of vacuous black: mere nothingness, resonating, existing only inside me, so that I was the entire, sham universe, the entire, dead void. I am the black hole which ate reality and made it this: a blank.

Her perfume:
The scent of love

And the scent
Of ruin.

You sowed seeds
In the ruined
Castles of my heart:

Spread flowers
Across the abandoned
Highways.

Even my footsteps
Seemed to echo
With the sound of

"What if?"

A Day Dream Haiku.

Drifting cotton clouds,
High in a day dreamer's sky
Carry me to you.

A Haiku in Bark.

Our names carved in bark,
A love as old as the trees,
Withers in winter.

She was

A sea, but I

Was just

A ripple.

Even time was
In love
With you.

It was always
Rushing and
Flying whenever
You were near.

But none
Of the paths
Lead back
To who
I used to be.

What pulled
Us apart? Was
It the hours,

The ticking of
The clock or
The changing of the
Seasons and the
Falling of the
Leaves?

What pulled
Us apart? And
Why do I still
Wait for you
And dream of
You in the
Silence after

The rain?

Lonely cars
Drive lonely roads
Under empty
Lights in an
Empty city and I

Turn on the
Radio, wind down
My window, listen to
The road call,
And think of
You, somewhere

Under these stars.

A Haiku at Dawn.

The moon sinks lower,
Dawn exhales across the sky,
But I miss my dreams.

"There is such majestic splendour when you are alone - broken at 4am. All is lost, there is no hope in the world and yet the sun is rising. The light is pale, diluted, but it will grow strong, and there will be a day time. All is lost, there is no hope in the world but there is another day at least, and another day is another chance."

Your kisses
Were a drop of
Water in this
Starving desert,

But you were
Only a mirage, and
What was left

Behind but a thirst
Even greater
Than before?

In her kisses
I tasted the ashes
Of burning stars
And vanished
Galaxies.

I have no memories

Before you.

It was a different place,

A different life,

And I was

A different person.

This is how
It ends:

With me
Clinging on
To a sinking
Ship in a

Dying dream
As the daylight
Calls.

How long can
You chase a dream
Until it becomes

A nightmare?

A Rainy Night.

Exhausted. Listening to the falling rain. Empty of emotion. Listening to the falling rain.

When we said
"How did we ever
Live before
Each other?"
I never expected
To say:

"How will I ever live
After you?"

And the heaviest
Weight of all
Is the pieces

Of a broken
Heart.

How strange that
A broken heart
Is heavier
Than a whole

One.

A dream is
Your heart
Telling
The truth.

After the storm
Comes the silence,
The loneliness,
And all of a sudden
I miss

The thunder.

Another night,
And I fall
Helplessly into
The arms of
A dream, wishing
It was
You.

A Summer Breeze Haiku.

The breeze through the leaves
Whispers a far off promise
Of you by my side.

We dreamed too
Much. Reality grew
Jealous and
Tore us apart.

Does the winter

Dream of the summer,

Just like I

Dream of you on

These dark

Nights?

Inside myself
I built a fortress.
Brick by brick,
Stone by stone,
And manned it
With archers and
Cannons and
Fire and pitch and
In the end
Not even I could
Escape, and
In the end not even
I could
Let anybody in.

We are already
Ghosts, hardly
Defined, hardly
Real. Our thoughts
Flicker and fade
In the dying
Embers of
The dawn.

It's a lie.
Sometimes numb
Is better.

I don't want
To love you.
I want
To be free,
I want
To be me,
But when I
Shut my eyes
All I see

is you.

I never thought
I would be the one
Missing

You.

How can there
Be an ocean
Between us?
We who were

the sea.

I went to that
Place inside my head
Where the stars
Go to die.

There are stories

In our atoms:

Poetry. The

Whispers and

The tales of the

Dying stars and

The births

Of galaxies.

We love
So easily, but

Break so
Easily
Too.

The doctors
Crowded round
And said:

"He lived too long
With her and
Could not live
Without."

Ups and downs
Are just the sea.
You need them
Both to reach
The shore.

And all I wish
Is to go back
To a time when
It was all ahead,
And not behind.

Even my footsteps
Seemed to echo
With the sound of
"What if?"

Let the snow
Fall. Hide my
Footsteps, bury
My heart:
I don't want
To remember

Anymore.

My heart on
My sleeve, and
Both unravelling.

Yes or
No: anything
But
"Maybe."

Where are
My dreams?
I search for them
In my sleep,
In the stars,
In poetry and
In stories but
I know, deep
Down, that they
Are in your eyes,
And lost forever.

But your words

Are still echoing

Every time I

Listen to

The silence.

There is no
Moon behind
Those clouds:
No stars, no sky,
Only clouds,
Only emptiness,

And behind my
Eyes there are
No dreams or
Hopes or loves,
But only wishes
For yesterday.

I'll burn my books
And silence my
Music. I'll stop
My pen and
Shut my eyes.

I don't want to feel
Any more.

Save as Draft.

I will come back
And try again
Later. Try again
Harder, or better,
And hope it will
Be enough
This time.

An Autumn Night Haiku.

Starry autumn sky,
Glimmers with pin prick wishes
That I spent on you.

I was never
Sure whether it
Was worth
Everything, or
Nothing
At all.

And I could
Never tell
Whether you
Were the dusk
Or the dawn:

The beginning
Or the end.

Amongst the
Shattered pieces
Of myself I
Began to find
Traces of you.

I have lost
Myself somewhere,
Searching
For you.

My heart
And mind
Are far older
Than my
Body.

The sea
Sweeps the
Shore and
The morning
Hides the
Stars,

But I am
Still wrapped
In memories.

I let myself
Drown, but found
I could breathe

Beneath
The waves.

I wrote

Your name

In the sands

Of my heart,

But the

Seas of

Yesterday

Swept it

Away.

Too many
Yesterdays and
Not enough
Tomorrows.

In the maze
Of my heart your
Ghost still
Stalks the passages,
The chambers and
The dusty stairs
Where spider's webs
Cling and trap
My every step.

In the maze
Of my heart your ghost
Is not alone, it
Walks side by side
With my own.

When will it
End? Your voice
Still whispers
To me in
My dreams.

I began to

Crack at the seams.

My thoughts

Groaned and strained,

Struggling for

The outside.

The sea was too
Strong. The shore
Too weak. All
The waves of you
Came battering
In, regardless
Of my cliffs and
Defences.

Does the moon
Miss the earth, as
It sits alone
Amongst the
Dying whispers
Of far flung stars?

I wish I had
Lived the life
I wrote about.

In your eyes
Did I see
The beginning
Or the end?

MORE BOOKS BY DAVID JONES.

Love & Space Dust. A Poetry Anthology.

Love & Space Dust is a poetry anthology exploring love and eternity. Timeless poetry of feeling and emotion, Love & Space Dust carries readers on a journey through love, life and relationships, and then far beyond, into the stars and the far flung galaxies, where all that remains of the feelings we once felt and the lives we once lived is love and space dust.

"After spending over ten years in a literature club and hearing/ reading more poems than I could count, I thought I had seen it all. I have never been so wrong. Love and Space Dust contains so many beautifully written poems that brought tears to my eyes that I didn't put my Kindle down until I had read every single one of them at least twice." Amazon.de Customer Review.

"Lovely book." Amazon.com Customer Review

"I really enjoy all of the poems. They make you feel like never before. By far some of my favorite poems." Amazon.com Customer Review.

"LOVED LOVED LOVED THIS!!" Goodreads Review.

"These poems are so full of Pain and Darkness, but so full of Hope and Light." Amazon.de Customer Review.

"This book is absolutely amazing and i hope there will be more to come!" Amazon.com Customer Review.

"Love this book so much!" Goodreads Review.

Could You Ever Live Without? A Poetry Anthology.

Poems of feeling and experience, the anthology encompasses all of life and beyond: death, the universe, hopes, dreams, love, loss - all of existence contained in one work. Poetry that captures both moments and lifetimes, memories and hopes, reality and dreams. Poems to identify with, poems of life.

"Take it from a non-poetry reader: this book is a gem, destined to become timeless." Amazon Customer Review.

"Loved the poems, a very great read. Once I started reading it was hard to stop." Amazon Customer Review.

"This book is beautiful. It's one of my most cherished possessions." Amazon Customer Review.

"Not all poetry is worth reading. This is." Amazon Customer Review.

"A great reflection of the deeper thoughts from this generation." Amazon Customer Review.

"Beautiful collection of poetry, I'm not an avid poetry reader but this book is absolutely stunning." Amazon.co.uk Customer Review.

"Everytime I read this book I find new meanings." Goodreads Review.

"Everyone should have a copy on their bookshelf." Amazon.com Customer Review.

Death's Door. A Novella.

"She was like the dawn, insubstantial and somehow transient, as though she would fade from reality at any moment."

Every day the villagers watch as Death, a spectral suit of black armour mounted upon a horse, rides through the valley beneath their mountain top home. After a lifetime living on the edge of Death's domain, his close proximity is neither terrible or threatening, rather he has become a simple fact of life and a familiar neighbour. Nothing seems to change until one night a young boy, alone in the meadows beneath a summer moon, watches a mysterious figure in white approaching the village through the tall grass.

"A spectacular novella, a quick read but engaging and thoughtful. The story carries you as swift as death's horse does." Amazon.com Customer Review.

"Buy this book! Great teen-based book. Even better for post teen (aka 55 year old father) reader." Amazon.com Customer Review.

"This book quickly became my forever favorite. You will not regret buying it. Although it's about death himself, it has so much to teach about life." Amazon.com Customer Review.

Love As The Stars Went Out. A Poetry Anthology.

A collection of poetry from the end of the world. Poems of love, feeling and emotion, the collection encompasses all of life, and even beyond. Simple and elegant, the book contains all the poetry of existence.

"This book is amazing I would really recommend getting the other two as well they are some of my favourite books of all time." Amazon.co.uk Customer Review.

"I love every bit of this book. So simple yet deep meaningful words. I would recommend it to all and everyone…." Amazon.com Customer Review.

"Five stars. Awesome book." Amazon.com Customer Review.

"Such a beautiful piece." Amazon.com Customer Review.

And Coming Soon...

A full length novel by David Jones exploring themes of love, eternity, the nature of the universe and history.

"When all of this is over, will our atoms play amongst the stars? Will we dance and laugh through the galaxies? Will we be happy at last?"

For further information and news on the novel please visit:

Twitter: @djthedavid
Instagram: @storydj
Youtube: youtube.com/storydj
Facebook: facebook.com/davidjoneswriter

Made in the USA
Columbia, SC
11 December 2017